POEMS

BY

WILLIAM VAUGHN MOODY

BOSTON AND NEW YORK
HOUGHTON, MIFFLIN AND COMPANY
The Riverside Press, Cambridge

NOTE

Several poems of this collection, including "An Ode in Time of Hesitation," "The Brute," and "On a Soldier Fallen in the Philippines," have appeared in the *Atlantic Monthly*; "Gloucester Moors" and "Faded Pictures," in *Scribner's Magazine*; and "The Ride Back," under a different title in the *Chap-Book*. The author is indebted to the editors of these periodicals for leave to reprint.

CONTENTS

POEMS

GLOUCESTER MOORS

A MILE behind is Gloucester town
Where the fishing fleets put in,
A mile ahead the land dips down
And the woods and farms begin.
Here, where the moors stretch free
In the high blue afternoon,
Are the marching sun and talking sea,
And the racing winds that wheel and flee
On the flying heels of June.

Jill-o'er-the-ground is purple blue,
Blue is the quaker-maid,
The wild geranium holds its dew
Long in the boulder's shade.
Wax-red hangs the cup
From the huckleberry boughs,
In barberry bells the grey moths sup,
Or where the choke-cherry lifts high up
Sweet bowls for their carouse.

Over the shelf of the sandy cove
Beach-peas blossom late.

By copse and cliff the swallows rove
Each calling to his mate.
Seaward the sea-gulls go,
And the land-birds all are here;
That green-gold flash was a vireo,
And yonder flame where the marsh-flags grow
Was a scarlet tanager.

This earth is not the steadfast place
We landsmen build upon;
From deep to deep she varies pace,
And while she comes is gone.
Beneath my feet I feel
Her smooth bulk heave and dip;
With velvet plunge and soft upreel
She swings and steadies to her keel
Like a gallant, gallant ship.

These summer clouds she sets for sail,
The sun is her masthead light,
She tows the moon like a pinnace frail
Where her phosphor wake churns bright.
Now hid, now looming clear,
On the face of the dangerous blue
The star fleets tack and wheel and veer,
But on, but on does the old earth steer
As if her port she knew.

God, dear God! Does she know her port,
Though she goes so far about?
Or blind astray, does she make her sport
To brazen and chance it out?
I watched when her captains passed:
She were better captainless.
Men in the cabin, before the mast,
But some were reckless and some aghast,
And some sat gorged at mess.

By her battened hatch I leaned and caught
Sounds from the noisome hold, —
Cursing and sighing of souls distraught
And cries too sad to be told.
Then I strove to go down and see;
But they said, "Thou art not of us!"
I turned to those on the deck with me
And cried, "Give help!" But they said, "Let be:
Our ship sails faster thus."

Jill-o'er-the-ground is purple blue,
Blue is the quaker-maid,
The alder-clump where the brook comes through
Breeds cresses in its shade.
To be out of the moiling street
With its swelter and its sin!

Who has given to me this sweet,
And given my brother dust to eat?
And when will his wage come in?

Scattering wide or blown in ranks,
Yellow and white and brown,
Boats and boats from the fishing banks
Come home to Gloucester town.
There is cash to purse and spend,
There are wives to be embraced,
Hearts to borrow and hearts to lend,
And hearts to take and keep to the end, —
O little sails, make haste!

But thou, vast outbound ship of souls,
What harbor town for thee?
What shapes, when thy arriving tolls,
Shall crowd the banks to see?
Shall all the happy shipmates then
Stand singing brotherly?
Or shall a haggard ruthless few
Warp her over and bring her to,
While the many broken souls of men
Fester down in the slaver's pen,
And nothing to say or do?

GOOD FRIDAY NIGHT

AT last the bird that sang so long
In twilight circles, hushed his song:
Above the ancient square
The stars came here and there.

Good Friday night! Some hearts were bowed,
But some amid the waiting crowd
Because of too much youth
Felt not that mystic ruth;

And of these hearts my heart was one:
Nor when beneath the arch of stone
With dirge and candle flame
The cross of passion came,

Did my glad spirit feel reproof,
Though on the awful tree aloof,
Unspiritual, dead,
Drooped the ensanguined Head.

To one who stood where myrtles made
A little space of deeper shade

(As I could half descry,
A stranger, even as I),

I said, "These youths who bear along
The symbols of their Saviour's wrong,
The spear, the garment torn,
The flaggel, and the thorn,—

"Why do they make this mummery?
Would not a brave man gladly die
For a much smaller thing
Than to be Christ and king?"

He answered nothing, and I turned.
Throned in its hundred candles burned
The jeweled eidolon
Of her who bore the Son.

The crowd was prostrate; still, I felt
No shame until the stranger knelt;
Then not to kneel, almost
Seemed like a vulgar boast.

I knelt. The doll-face, waxen white,
Flowered out a living dimness; bright
Dawned the dear mortal grace
Of my own mother's face.

When we were risen up, the street
Was vacant; all the air hung sweet
With lemon-flowers; and soon
The sky would hold the moon.

More silently than new-found friends
To whom much silence makes amends
For the much babble vain
While yet their lives were twain,

We walked along the odorous hill.
The light was little yet; his will
I could not see to trace
Upon his form or face.

So when aloft the gold moon broke,
I cried, heart-stung. As one who woke
He turned unto my cries
The anguish of his eyes.

"Friend! Master!" I cried falteringly,
"Thou seest the thing they make of thee.
Oh, by the light divine
My mother shares with thine,

"I beg that I may lay my head
Upon thy shoulder and be fed

With thoughts of brotherhood!"
So through the odorous wood,

More silently than friends new-found
We walked. At the first meadow bound
His figure ashen-stoled
Sank in the moon's broad gold.

ROAD-HYMN FOR THE START

LEAVE the early bells at chime,
Leave the kindled hearth to blaze,
Leave the trellised panes where children linger out the waking-time,
Leave the forms of sons and fathers trudging through the misty ways,
Leave the sounds of mothers taking up their sweet laborious days.

Pass them by! even while our soul
Yearns to them with keen distress.
Unto them a part is given; we will strive to see the whole.
Dear shall be the banquet table where their singing spirits press;
Dearer be our sacred hunger, and our pilgrim loneliness.

We have felt the ancient swaying
Of the earth before the sun,
On the darkened marge of midnight heard sidereal rivers playing;

Rash it was to bathe our souls there, but we
plunged and all was done.
That is lives and lives behind us — lo, our journey is begun!

Careless where our face is set,
Let us take the open way.
What we are no tongue has told us: Errand-goers who forget?
Soldiers heedless of their harry? Pilgrim people
gone astray?
We have heard a voice cry "Wander!" That
was all we heard it say.

Ask no more: 't is much, 't is much!
Down the road the day-star calls;
Touched with change in the wide heavens, like a
leaf the frost winds touch,
Flames the failing moon a moment, ere it shrivels
white and falls;
Hid aloft, a wild throat holdeth sweet and sweeter
intervals.

Leave him still to ease in song
Half his little heart's unrest:
Speech is his, but we may journey toward the life
for which we long.

God, who gives the bird its anguish, maketh nothing manifest,
But upon our lifted foreheads pours the boon of endless quest.

AN ODE IN TIME OF HESITATION

(After seeing at Boston the statue of Robert Gould Shaw, killed while storming Fort Wagner, July 18, 1863, at the head of the first enlisted negro regiment, the 54th Massachusetts.)

I

BEFORE the solemn bronze Saint Gaudens made
To thrill the heedless passer's heart with awe,
And set here in the city's talk and trade
To the good memory of Robert Shaw,
This bright March morn I stand,
And hear the distant spring come up the land;
Knowing that what I hear is not unheard
Of this boy soldier and his negro band,
For all their gaze is fixed so stern ahead,
For all the fatal rhythm of their tread.
The land they died to save from death and shame
Trembles and waits, hearing the spring's great
name,
And by her pangs these resolute ghosts are stirred.

II

Through street and mall the tides of people go
Heedless; the trees upon the Common show

No hint of green; but to my listening heart
The still earth doth impart
Assurance of her jubilant emprise,
And it is clear to my long-searching eyes
That love at last has might upon the skies.
The ice is runneled on the little pond;
A telltale patter drips from off the trees;
The air is touched with southland spiceries,
As if but yesterday it tossed the frond
Of pendent mosses where the live-oaks grow
Beyond Virginia and the Carolines,
Or had its will among the fruits and vines
Of aromatic isles asleep beyond
Florida and the Gulf of Mexico.

III

Soon shall the Cape Ann children shout in glee,
Spying the arbutus, spring's dear recluse;
Hill lads at dawn shall hearken the wild goose
Go honking northward over Tennessee;
West from Oswego to Sault Sainte-Marie,
And on to where the Pictured Rocks are hung,
And yonder where, gigantic, willful, young,
Chicago sitteth at the northwest gates,
With restless violent hands and casual tongue
Moulding her mighty fates,
The Lakes shall robe them in ethereal sheen;

And like a larger sea, the vital green
Of springing wheat shall vastly be outflung
Over Dakota and the prairie states.
By desert people immemorial
On Arizonan mesas shall be done
Dim rites unto the thunder and the sun;
Nor shall the primal gods lack sacrifice
More splendid, when the white Sierras call
Unto the Rockies straightway to arise
And dance before the unveiled ark of the year,
Sounding their windy cedars as for shawms,
Unrolling rivers clear
For flutter of broad phylacteries;
While Shasta signals to Alaskan seas
That watch old sluggish glaciers downward creep
To fling their icebergs thundering from the steep,
And Mariposa through the purple calms
Gazes at far Hawaii crowned with palms
Where East and West are met, —
A rich seal on the ocean's bosom set
To say that East and West are twain,
With different loss and gain:
The Lord hath sundered them; let them be sundered yet.

IV

Alas! what sounds are these that come
Sullenly over the Pacific seas, —

Sounds of ignoble battle, striking dumb
The season's half-awakened ecstasies ?
Must I be humble, then,
Now when my heart hath need of pride ?
Wild love falls on me from these sculptured men ;
By loving much the land for which they died
I would be justified.
My spirit was away on pinions wide
To soothe in praise of her its passionate mood
And ease it of its ache of gratitude.
Too sorely heavy is the debt they lay
On me and the companions of my day.
I would remember now
My country's goodliness, make sweet her name.
Alas ! what shade art thou
Of sorrow or of blame
Liftest the lyric leafage from her brow,
And pointest a slow finger at her shame ?

V

Lies ! lies ! It cannot be ! The wars we wage
Are noble, and our battles still are won
By justice for us, ere we lift the gage.
We have not sold our loftiest heritage.
The proud republic hath not stooped to cheat
And scramble in the market-place of war ;
Her forehead weareth yet its solemn star.

Here is her witness: this, her perfect son,
This delicate and proud New England soul
Who leads despisèd men, with just-unshackled feet,
Up the large ways where death and glory meet,
To show all peoples that our shame is done,
That once more we are clean and spirit-whole.

VI

Crouched in the sea fog on the moaning sand
All night he lay, speaking some simple word
From hour to hour to the slow minds that heard,
Holding each poor life gently in his hand
And breathing on the base rejected clay
Till each dark face shone mystical and grand
Against the breaking day;
And lo, the shard the potter cast away
Was grown a fiery chalice crystal-fine
Fulfilled of the divine
Great wine of battle wrath by God's ring-finger stirred.
Then upward, where the shadowy bastion loomed
Huge on the mountain in the wet sea light,
Whence now, and now, infernal flowerage bloomed,
Bloomed, burst, and scattered down its deadly seed,—
They swept, and died like freemen on the height,

Like freemen, and like men of noble breed;
And when the battle fell away at night
By hasty and contemptuous hands were thrust
Obscurely in a common grave with him
The fair-haired keeper of their love and trust.
Now limb doth mingle with dissolvèd limb
In nature's busy old democracy
To flush the mountain laurel when she blows
Sweet by the southern sea,
And heart with crumbled heart climbs in the rose: —
The untaught hearts with the high heart that knew
This mountain fortress for no earthly hold
Of temporal quarrel, but the bastion old
Of spiritual wrong,
Built by an unjust nation sheer and strong,
Expugnable but by a nation's rue
And bowing down before that equal shrine
By all men held divine,
Whereof his band and he were the most holy sign.

VII

O bitter, bitter shade!
Wilt thou not put the scorn
And instant tragic question from thine eyes?
Do thy dark brows yet crave
That swift and angry stave —

Unmeet for this desirous morn —
That I have striven, striven to evade?
Gazing on him, must I not deem they err
Whose careless lips in street and shop aver
As common tidings, deeds to make his cheek
Flush from the bronze, and his dead throat to speak?
Surely some elder singer would arise,
Whose harp hath leave to threaten and to mourn
Above this people when they go astray.
Is Whitman, the strong spirit, overworn?
Has Whittier put his yearning wrath away?
I will not and I dare not yet believe!
Though furtively the sunlight seems to grieve,
And the spring-laden breeze
Out of the gladdening west is sinister
With sounds of nameless battle overseas;
Though when we turn and question in suspense
If these things be indeed after these ways,
And what things are to follow after these,
Our fluent men of place and consequence
Fumble and fill their mouths with hollow phrase,
Or for the end-all of deep arguments
Intone their dull commercial liturgies —
I dare not yet believe! My ears are shut!
I will not hear the thin satiric praise
And muffled laughter of our enemies,

Bidding us never sheathe our valiant sword
Till we have changed our birthright for a gourd
Of wild pulse stolen from a barbarian's hut;
Showing how wise it is to cast away
The symbols of our spiritual sway,
That so our hands with better ease
May wield the driver's whip and grasp the jailer's
keys.

VIII

Was it for this our fathers kept the law?
This crown shall crown their struggle and their
ruth?
Are we the eagle nation Milton saw
Mewing its mighty youth,
Soon to possess the mountain winds of truth,
And be a swift familiar of the sun
Where aye before God's face his trumpets run?
Or have we but the talons and the maw,
And for the abject likeness of our heart
Shall some less lordly bird be set apart?—
Some gross-billed wader where the swamps are
fat?
Some gorger in the sun? Some prowler with the
bat?

IX

Ah no!
We have not fallen so.

We are our fathers' sons: let those who lead us
know!
'T was only yesterday sick Cuba's cry
Came up the tropic wind, "Now help us, for we
die!"
Then Alabama heard,
And rising, pale, to Maine and Idaho
Shouted a burning word.
Proud state with proud impassioned state con-
ferred,
And at the lifting of a hand sprang forth,
East, west, and south, and north,
Beautiful armies. Oh, by the sweet blood and
young
Shed on the awful hill slope at San Juan,
By the unforgotten names of eager boys
Who might have tasted girls' love and been
stung
With the old mystic joys
And starry griefs, now the spring nights come on,
But that the heart of youth is generous, —
We charge you, ye who lead us,
Breathe on their chivalry no hint of stain!
Turn not their new-world victories to gain!
One least leaf plucked for chaffer from the bays
Of their dear praise,
One jot of their pure conquest put to hire,
The implacable republic will require;

With clamor, in the glare and gaze of noon,
Or subtly, coming as a thief at night,
But surely, very surely, slow or soon
That insult deep we deeply will requite.
Tempt not our weakness, our cupidity!
For save we let the island men go free,
Those baffled and dislaureled ghosts
Will curse us from the lamentable coasts
Where walk the frustrate dead.
The cup of trembling shall be drainèd quite,
Eaten the sour bread of astonishment,
With ashes of the hearth shall be made white
Our hair, and wailing shall be in the tent;
Then on your guiltier head
Shall our intolerable self-disdain
Wreak suddenly its anger and its pain;
For manifest in that disastrous light
We shall discern the right
And do it, tardily. — O ye who lead,
Take heed!
Blindness we may forgive, but baseness we will
smite.

1900.

THE QUARRY

BETWEEN the rice swamps and the fields of tea
I met a sacred elephant, snow-white.
Upon his back a huge pagoda towered
Full of brass gods and food of sacrifice.
Upon his forehead sat a golden throne,
The massy metal twisted into shapes
Grotesque, antediluvian, such as move
In myth or have their broken images
Sealed in the stony middle of the hills.
A peacock spread his thousand dyes to screen
The yellow sunlight from the head of one
Who sat upon the throne, clad stiff with gems,
Heirlooms of dynasties of buried kings, —
Himself the likeness of a buried king,
With frozen gesture and unfocused eyes.
The trappings of the beast were over-scrawled
With broideries — sea-shapes and flying things,
Fan-trees and dwarfed nodosities of pine,
Mixed with old alphabets, and faded lore
Fallen from ecstatic mouths before the Flood,
Or gathered by the daughters when they walked
Eastward in Eden with the Sons of God
Whom love and the deep moon made garrulous.

Between the carven tusks his trunk hung dead;
Blind as the eyes of pearl in Buddha's brow
His beaded eyes stared thwart upon the road;
And feebler than the doting knees of eld,
His joints, of size to swing the builder's crane
Across the war-walls of the Anakim,
Made vain and shaken haste. Good need was his
To hasten: panting, foaming, on the slot
Came many brutes of prey, their several hates
Laid by until the sharing of the spoil.
Just as they gathered stomach for the leap,
The sun was darkened, and wide-balanced wings
Beat downward on the trade-wind from the sea.
A wheel of shadow sped along the fields
And o'er the dreaming cities. Suddenly
My heart misgave me, and I cried aloud,
"Alas! What dost thou here? What dost *thou* here?"
The great beasts and the little halted sharp,
Eyed the grand circler, doubting his intent.
Straightway the wind flawed and he came about,
Stooping to take the vanward of the pack;
Then turned, between the chasers and the chased,
Crying a word I could not understand,—
But stiller-tongued, with eyes somewhat askance,
They settled to the slot and disappeared.

1900.

ON A SOLDIER FALLEN IN THE PHILIPPINES

STREETS of the roaring town,
Hush for him, hush, be still!
He comes, who was stricken down
Doing the word of our will.
Hush! Let him have his state,
Give him his soldier's crown.
The grists of trade can wait
Their grinding at the mill,
But he cannot wait for his honor, now the trumpet has been blown.
Wreathe pride now for his granite brow, lay love on his breast of stone.

Toll! Let the great bells toll
Till the clashing air is dim.
Did we wrong this parted soul?
We will make it up to him.
Toll! Let him never guess
What work we set him to.
Laurel, laurel, yes;
He did what we bade him do.

Praise, and never a whispered hint but the fight
he fought was good;
Never a word that the blood on his sword was
his country's own heart's-blood.

A flag for the soldier's bier
Who dies that his land may live;
O, banners, banners here,
That he doubt not nor misgive!
That he heed not from the tomb
The evil days draw near
When the nation, robed in gloom,
With its faithless past shall strive.
Let him never dream that his bullet's scream
went wide of its island mark,
Home to the heart of his darling land where she
stumbled and sinned in the dark.

UNTIL THE TROUBLING OF THE WATERS

Two hours, two hours: God give me strength
 for it!
He who has given so much strength to me
And nothing to my child, must give to-day
What more I need to try and save my child
And get for him the life I owe to him.
To think that I may get it for him now,
Before he knows how much he might have
 missed
That other boys have got! The bitterest thought
Of all that plagued me when he came was this,
How some day he would see the difference,
And drag himself to me with puzzled eyes
To ask me why it was. He would have been
Cruel enough to do it, knowing not
That was the question my rebellious heart
Cried over and over one whole year to God,
And got no answer and no help at all.
If he had asked me, what could I have said?
What single word could I have found to say
To hide me from his searching, puzzled gaze?

Some coward thing at best, never the truth;
The truth I never could have told him. No,
I never could have said, "God gave you me
To fashion you a body, right and strong,
With sturdy little limbs and chest and neck
For fun and fighting with your little mates,
Great feats and voyages in the breathless world
Of out-of-doors, — He gave you me for this,
And I was such a bungler, that is all!"
O, the old lie — that thought was not the worst.
I never have been truthful with myself.
For by the door where lurked one ghostly thought
I stood with crazy hands to thrust it back
If it should dare to peep and whisper out
Unbearable things about me, hearing which
The women passing in the streets would turn
To pity me and scold me with their eyes,
Who was so bad a mother and so slow
To learn to help God do his wonder in her
That she — O my sweet baby! It was not
The fear that you would see the difference
Between you and the other boys and girls;
No, no, it was the dimmer, wilder fear,
That you might never see it, never look
Out of your tiny baby-house of mind,
But sit your life through, quiet in the dark,
Smiling and nodding at what was not there!

A foolish fear: God could not punish so.
Yet until yesterday I thought He would.
My soul was always cowering at the blow
I saw suspended, ready to be dealt
The moment that I showed my fear too much.
Therefore I hid it from Him all I could,
And only stole a shaking glance at it
Sometimes in the dead minutes before dawn
When He forgets to watch. Till yesterday.
For yesterday was wonderful and strange
From the beginning. When I wakened first
And looked out at the window, the last snow
Was gone from earth; about the apple-trees
Hung a faint mist of bloom; small sudden green
Had run and spread and rippled everywhere
Over the fields; and in the level sun
Walked something like a presence and a power,
Uttering hopes and loving-kindnesses
To all the world, but chiefly unto me.
It walked before me when I went to work,
And all day long the noises of the mill
Were spun upon a core of golden sound,
Half-spoken words and interrupted songs
Of blessed promise, meant for all the world,
But most for me, because I suffered most.
The shooting spindles, the smooth-humming
wheels,

The rocking webs, seemed toiling to some end
Beneficent and human known to them,
And duly brought to pass in power and love.
The faces of the girls and men at work
Met mine with intense greeting, veiled at once,
As if they knew a secret they must keep
For fear the joy would harm me if they told
Before some inkling filtered to my mind
In roundabout ways. When the day's work was
done
There lay a special silence on the fields;
And, as I passed, the bushes and the trees,
The very ruts and puddles of the road
Spoke to each other, saying it was she,
The happy woman, the elected one,
The vessel of strange mercy and the sign
Of many loving wonders done in Heaven
To help the piteous earth.

At last I stopped
And looked about me in sheer wonderment.
What did it mean? What did they want with
me?
What was the matter with the evening now
That it was just as bound to make me glad
As morning and the live-long day had been?
Me, who had quite forgot what gladness was,

Who had no right to anything but toil,
And food and sleep for strength to toil again,
And that fierce frightened anguish of my love
For the poor little spirit I had wronged
With life that was no life. What had befallen
Since yesterday? No need to stop and ask!
Back there in the dark places of my mind
Where I had thrust it, fearing to believe
An unbelievable mercy, shone the news
Told by the village neighbors coming home
Last night from the great city, of a man
Arisen, like the first evangelists,
With power to heal the bodies of the sick,
In testimony of his master Christ,
Who heals the soul when it is sick with sin.
Could such a thing be true in these hard days?
Was help still sent in such a way as that?
No, no! I did not dare to think of it,
Feeling what weakness and despair would come
After the crazy hope broke under me.
I turned and started homeward, faster now,
But never fast enough to leave behind
The voices and the troubled happiness
That still kept mounting, mounting like a sea,
And singing far-off like a rush of wings.
Far down the road a yellow spot of light
Shone from my cottage window, rayless yet,

Where the last sunset crimson caught the panes.
Alice had lit the lamp before she went;
Her day of pity and unmirthful play
Was over, and her young heart free to live
Until to-morrow brought her nursing-task
Again, and made her feel how dark and still
That life could be to others which to her
Was full of dreams that beckoned, reaching hands,
And thrilling invitations young girls hear.
My boy was sleeping, little mind and frame
More tired just lying there awake two hours
Than with a whole day's romp he should have
been.
He would not know his mother had come home;
But after supper I would sit awhile
Beside his bed, and let my heart have time
For that worst love that stabs and breaks and kills.
This I thought over to myself by rote
And habit, but I could not feel my thoughts;
For still that dim unmeaning happiness
Kept mounting, mounting round me like a sea,
And singing inward like a wind of wings.

Before I lifted up the latch, I knew.
I felt no fear; the One who waited there
In the low lamplight by the bed, had come
Because I was his sister and in need.

My word had got to Him somehow at last,
And He had come to help me or to tell
Where help was to be found. It was not strange.
Strange only He had stayed away so long;
But that should be forgotten — He was here.
I pushed the door wide open and looked in.
He had been kneeling by the bed, and now,
Half-risen, kissed my boy upon the lips,
Then turned and smiled and pointed with his hand.
I must have fallen on the threshold stone,
For I remember that I felt, not saw,
The resurrection glory and the peace
Shed from his face and raiment as He went
Out by the door into the evening street.
But when I looked, the place about the bed
Was yet all bathed in light, and in the midst
My boy lay changed, — no longer clothed upon
With scraps and shreds of life, but like the child
Of some most fortunate mother. In a breath
The image faded. There he lay again
The same as always; and the light was gone.
I sank with moans and cries beside the bed.
The cruelty, O Christ, the cruelty!
To come at last and then to go like that,
Leaving the darkness deeper than before!

Then, though I heard no sound, I grew aware
Of some one standing by the open door
Among the dry vines rustling in the porch.
My heart laughed suddenly. He had come back!
He had come back to make the vision true.
He had not meant to mock me: God was God,
And Christ was Christ; there was no falsehood
there.
I heard a quiet footstep cross the room
And felt a hand laid gently on my hair,—
A human hand, worn hard by daily toil,
Heavy with life-long struggle after bread.
Alice's father. The kind homely voice
Had in it such strange music that I dreamed
Perhaps it was the Other speaking in him,
Because His own bright form had made me swoon
With its too much of glory. What he brought
Was news as good as ever heavenly lips
Had the dear right to utter. He had been
All day among the crowds of curious folk
From the great city and the country-side
Gathered to watch the Healer do his work
Of mercy on the sick and halt and blind,
And with his very eyes had seen such things
As awestruck men had witnessed long ago
In Galilee, and writ of in the Book.
To-morrow morning he would take me there

If I had strength and courage to believe.
It might be there was hope; he could not say,
But knew what he had seen. When he was gone
I lay for hours, letting the solemn waves
Thundering joy go over and over me.

Just before midnight baby fretted, woke;
He never yet has slept a whole night through
Without his food and petting. As I sat
Feeding and petting him and singing soft,
I felt a jealousy begin to ache
And worry at my heartstrings, hushing down
The gladness. Jealousy of what or whom?
I hardly knew, or could not put in words;
At least it seemed too foolish and too wrong
When said, and so I shut the thought away.
Only, next minute, it came stealing back.
After the change, would my boy be the same
As this one? Would he be my boy at all,
And not another's — his who gave the life
I could not give, or did not anyhow?
How could I look in his new eyes to claim
The whole of him, the body and the breath,
When some one not his mother, a strange man,
Had clothed him in that beauty of the flesh —
Perhaps (for who could know?), perhaps, by some
Hateful disfiguring miracle, had even

Transformed his spirit to a better one,
Better, but not the same I prayed for him
Down out of Heaven through the sleepless
nights, —
The best that God would send to such as me.
I tried to strangle back the wicked pain;
Fancied him changed and tried to love him so.
No use; it was another, not my child,
Not my frail, broken, priceless little one,
My cup of anguish, and my trembling star
Hung small and sad and sweet above the earth,
So sure to fall but for my cherishing!

When he had dropped asleep again, I rose
And wrestled with the sinful selfishness,
The dark injustice, the unnatural pain.
Fevered at last with pacing to and fro,
I raised the bedroom window and leaned out.
The white moon, low behind the sycamores,
Silvered the silent country; not a voice
Of all the myriads summer moves to sing
Had yet awakened; in the level moon
Walked that same presence I had heard at dawn
Uttering hopes and loving-kindnesses,
But now, dispirited and reticent,
It walked the moonlight like a homeless thing.
O, how to cleanse me of the cowardice!

How to be just! Was I a mother, then,
A mother, and not love her child as well
As her own covetous and morbid love?
Was it for this the Comforter had come,
Smiling at me and pointing with His hand?
—What had He meant to have me think or do,
Smiling and pointing?

All at once I saw
A way to save my darling from myself
And make atonement for my grudging love!
Under the sycamores and up the hill
And down across the river, the wet road
Went stretching cityward, silvered in the moon.
I who had shrunk from sacrifice, even I,
Who had refused God's blessing for my boy,
Would take him in my arms and carry him
Up to the altar of the miracle.
I would not wait for daylight, nor the help
Of any human friendship; I alone,
Through the still miles of country, I alone,
Only my arms to shield him and my feet
To bear him: he should have no one to thank
But me for that. I knew the way was long,
But knew strength would be given. So I came.
Soon the stars failed; the late moon faded too:
I think my heart had sucked their beams from them

To build more blue amid the murky night
Its own miraculous day. From creeks and fields
The fog climbed slowly, blotted out the road;
And hid the signposts telling of the town;
After a while rain fell, with sleet and snow.
What did I care? Baby was snug and dry.
Some day, when I was telling him of this,
He would but hug me closer, hearing how
The night conspired against us. Better hard
Than easy, then: I almost felt regret
My body was so capable and strong
To do its errand. Honeyed drop by drop,
The ghostly jealousy, loosening at my breast,
Distilled into a dew of quiet tears
And fell with splash of music in the wells
And on the hidden rivers of my soul.

The hardest part was coming through the town.
The country, even when it hindered most,
Seemed conscious of the thing I went to find.
The rocks and bushes looming through the mist
Questioned and acquiesced and understood;
The trees and streams believed; the wind and rain,
Even they, for all their temper, had some words
Of faith and comfort. But the glaring streets,
The dizzy traffic, the piled merchandise,

The giant buildings swarming with fierce life —
Cared nothing for me. They had never heard
Of me nor of my business. When I asked
My way, a shade of pity or contempt
Showed through men's kindness — for they all
 were kind.
Daunted and chilled and very sick at heart,
I walked the endless pavements. But at last
The streets grew quieter; the houses seemed
As if they might be homes where people lived;
Then came the factories and cottages,
And all was well again. Much more than well,
For many sick and broken went my way,
Alone or helped along by loving hands;
And from a thousand eyes the famished hope
Looked out at mine — wild, patient, querulous,
But always hope and hope, a thousand tongues
Speaking one word in many languages.

In two hours He will come, they say, will stand
There on the steps, above the waiting crowd,
And touch with healing hands whoever asks
Believingly, in spirit and in truth.
Can such a mercy be, in these hard days?
Is help still sent in such a way as that?
Christ, I believe; pity my unbelief!

JETSAM

I WONDER can this be the world it was
At sunset? I remember the sky fell
Green as pale meadows, at the long street-ends,
But overhead the smoke-wrack hugged the roofs
As if to shut the city from God's eyes
Till dawn should quench the laughter and the
lights.
Beneath the gas flare stolid faces passed,
Too dull for sin; old loosened lips set hard
To drain the stale lees from the cup of sense;
Or if a young face yearned from out the mist
Made by its own bright hair, the eyes were wan
With desolate fore-knowledge of the end.
My life lay waste about me: as I walked,
From the gross dark of unfrequented streets
The face of my own youth peered forth at me,
Struck white with pity at the thing I was;
And globed in ghostly fire, thrice-virginal,
With lifted face star-strong, went one who sang
Lost verses from my youth's gold canticle.
Out of the void dark came my face and hers
One vivid moment — then the street was there;

Bloat shapes and mean eyes blotted the sear dusk;
And in the curtained window of a house
Whence sin reeked on the night, a shameful head
Was silhouetted black as Satan's face
Against eternal fires. I stumbled on
Down the dark slope that reaches riverward,
Stretching blind hands to find the throat of God
And crush Him in his lies. The river lay
Coiled in its factory filth and few lean trees.
All was too hateful — I could not die there!
I whom the Spring had strained unto her breast,
Whose lips had felt the wet vague lips of dawn.
So under the thin willows' leprous shade
And through the tangled ranks of riverweed
I pushed — till lo, God heard me! I came forth
Where, 'neath the shoreless hush of region light,
Through a new world, undreamed of, undesired,
Beyond imagining of man's weary heart,
Far to the white marge of the wondering sea
This still plain widens, and this moon rains down
Insufferable ecstasy of peace.

My heart is man's heart, strong to bear this night's
Unspeakable affliction of mute love
That crazes lesser things. The rocks and clods
Dissemble, feign a busy intercourse;
The bushes deal in shadowy subterfuge,

Lurk dull, dart spiteful out, make heartless signs,
Utter awestricken purpose of no sense, —
But I walk quiet, crush aside the hands
Stretched furtively to drag me madmen's ways.
I know the thing they suffer, and the tricks
They must be at to help themselves endure.
I would not be too boastful; I am weak,
Too weak to put aside the utter ache
Of this lone splendor long enough to see
Whether the moon is still her white strange self
Or something whiter, stranger, even the face
Which by the changed face of my risen youth
Sang, globed in fire, her golden canticle.
I dare not look again; another gaze
Might drive me to the wavering coppice there,
Where bat-winged madness brushed me, the wild laugh
Of naked nature crashed across my blood.
So rank it was with earthy presences,
Faun-shapes in goatish dance, young witches' eyes
Slanting deep invitation, whinnying calls
Ambiguous, shocks and whirlwinds of wild mirth, —
They had undone me in the darkness there,
But that within me, smiting through my lids
Lowered to shut in the thick whirl of sense,
The dumb light ached and rummaged, and without,

The soaring splendor summoned me aloud
To leave the low dank thickets of the flesh
Where man meets beast and makes his lair with
him,
For spirit reaches of the strenuous vast,
Where stalwart stars reap grain to make the bread
God breaketh at his tables and is glad.
I came out in the moonlight cleansed and strong,
And gazed up at the lyric face to see
All sweetness tasted of in earthen cups
Ere it be dashed and spilled, all radiance flung
Beyond experience, every benison dream,
Treasured and mystically crescent there.

O, who will shield me from her? Who will
place
A veil between me and the fierce in-throng
Of her inexorable benedicite?
See, I have loved her well and been with her!
Through tragic twilights when the stricken sea
Groveled with fear; or when she made her
throne
In imminent cities built of gorgeous winds
And paved with lightnings; or when the sobering
stars
Would lead her home 'mid wealth of plundered
May

Along the violet slopes of evensong.
Of all the sights that starred the dreamy year,
For me one sight stood peerless and apart:
Bright rivers tacit; low hills prone and dumb;
Forests that hushed their tiniest voice to hear;
Skies for the unutterable advent robed
In purple like the opening iris buds;
And by some lone expectant pool, one tree
Whose gray boughs shivered with excess of awe, —
As with preluding gush of amber light,
And herald trumpets softly lifted through,
Across the palpitant horizon marge
Crocus-filleted came the singing moon.
Out of her changing lights I wove my youth
A place to dwell in, sweet and spiritual,
And all the bitter years of my exile
My heart has called afar off unto her.
Lo, after many days love finds its own!
The futile adorations, the waste tears,
The hymns that fluttered low in the false dawn,
She has uptreasured as a lover's gifts;
They are the mystic garment that she wears
Against the bridal, and the crocus flowers
She twined her brow with at the going forth;
They are the burden of the song she made
In coming through the quiet fields of space,

And breathe between her passion-parted lips
Calling me out along the flowering road
Which summers through the dimness of the sea.

Hark, where the deep feels round its thousand
shores
To find remembered respite, and far drawn
Through weed-strewn shelves and crannies of the
coast
The myriad silence yearns to myriad speech.
O sea that yearns a day, shall thy tongues be
So eloquent, and heart, shall all thy tongues
Be dumb to speak thy longing? Say I hold
Life as a broken jewel in my hand,
And fain would buy a little love with it
For comfort, say I fain would make it shine
Once in remembering eyes ere it be dust, —
Were life not worthy spent? Then what of this,
When all my spirit hungers to repay
The beauty that has drenched my soul with
peace?
Once at a simple turning of the way
I met God walking; and although the dawn
Was large behind Him, and the morning stars
Circled and sang about his face as birds
About the fieldward morning cottager,
My coward heart said faintly, "Let us haste!

Day grows and it is far to market-town."
Once where I lay in darkness after fight,
Sore smitten, thrilled a little thread of song
Searching and searching at my muffled sense
Until it shook sweet pangs through all my blood,
And I beheld one globed in ghostly fire
Singing, star-strong, her golden canticle;
And her mouth sang, "The hosts of Hate roll past,
A dance of dust motes in the sliding sun;
Love's battle comes on the wide wings of storm,
From east to west one legion! Wilt thou strive?"
Then, since the splendor of her sword-bright gaze
Was heavy on me with yearning and with scorn
My sick heart muttered, "Yea, the little strife,
Yet see, the grievous wounds! I fain would sleep."
O heart, shalt thou not once be strong to go
Where all sweet throats are calling, once be brave
To slake with deed thy dumbness? Let us go
The path her singing face looms low to point,
Pendulous, blanched with longing, shedding flame
Of silver on the brown grope of the flood;
For all my spirit's soilure is put by
And all my body's soilure, lacking now
But the last lustral sacrament of death
To make me clean for those near-searching eyes

That question yonder whether all be well,
And pause a little ere they dare rejoice.

Question and be thou answered, passionate face!
For I am worthy, worthy now at last
After so long unworth; strong now at last
To give myself to beauty and be saved;
Now, being man, to give myself to thee,
As once the tumult of my boyish heart
Companioned thee with rapture through the world,
Forth from a land whereof no poet's lip
Made mention how the leas were lily-sprent,
Into a land God's eyes had looked not on
To love the tender bloom upon the hills.
To-morrow, when the fishers come at dawn
Upon that shell of me the sea has tossed
To land, as fit for earth to use again,
Men, meeting at the shops and corner streets,
Will speak a word of pity, glossing o'er
With altered accent, dubious sweep of hand,
Their virile, just contempt for one who failed.
But they can never cast my earnings up,
Who know so well my losses. Even you
Who in the mild light of the spirit walk
And hold yourselves acquainted with the truth,
Be not too swift to judge and cast me out!
You shall find other, nobler ways than mine

To work your soul's redemption, — glorious noons
Of battle 'neath the heaven-suspended sign,
And nightly refuge 'neath God's ægis-rim;
Increase of wisdom, and acquaintance held
With the heart's austerities; still governance,
And ripening of the blood in the weekday sun
To make the full-orbed consecrated fruit
At life's end for the Sabbath supper meet.
I shall not sit beside you at that feast,
For ere a seedling of my golden tree
Pushed off its petals to get room to grow,
I stripped the boughs to make an April gaud
And wreathe a spendthrift garland for my hair.
But mine is not the failure God deplores;
For I of old am beauty's votarist,
Long recreant, often foiled and led astray,
But resolute at last to seek her there
Where most she does abide, and crave with tears
That she assoil me of my blemishment.
Low looms her singing face to point the way,
Pendulous, blanched with longing, shedding flame
Of silver on the brown grope of the flood..
The stars are for me; the horizon wakes
Its pilgrim chanting; and the little sand
Grows musical of hope beneath my feet.
The waves that leap to meet my swimming breast
Gossip sweet secrets of the light-drenched way,

And when the deep throbs of the rising surge
Pulse upward with me, and a rain of wings
Blurs round the moon's pale place, she stoops to reach
Still welcome of bright hands across the wave,
And sings low, low, globed all in ghostly fire,
Lost verses from my youth's gold canticle.

THE BRUTE

THROUGH his might men work their wills.
They have boweled out the hills
For food to keep him toiling in the cages they have wrought;
And they fling him, hour by hour,
Limbs of men to give him power;
Brains of men to give him cunning; and for dainties to devour
Children's souls, the little worth; hearts of women, cheaply bought:
He takes them and he breaks them, but he gives them scanty thought.

For about the noisy land,
Roaring, quivering 'neath his hand,
His thoughts brood fierce and sullen or laugh in lust of pride
O'er the stubborn things that he,
Breaks to dust and brings to be.
Some he mightily establishes, some flings down utterly.

There is thunder in his stride, nothing ancient can abide,
When he hales the hills together and bridles up the tide.

Quietude and loveliness,
Holy sights that heal and bless,
They are scattered and abolished where his iron hoof is set;
When he splashes through the brae
Silver streams are choked with clay,
When he snorts the bright cliffs crumble and the woods go down like hay;
He lairs in pleasant cities, and the haggard people fret
Squalid 'mid their new-got riches, soot-begrimed and desolate.

They who caught and bound him tight
Laughed exultant at his might,
Saying, "Now behold, the good time comes for the weariest and the least!
We will use this lusty knave:
No more need for men to slave;
We may rise and look about us and have knowledge ere the grave."

But the Brute said in his breast, "Till the mills
I grind have ceased,
The riches shall be dust of dust, dry ashes be the
feast!

"On the strong and cunning few
Cynic favors I will strew;
I will stuff their maw with overplus until their
spirit dies;
From the patient and the low
I will take the joys they know;
They shall hunger after vanities and still an-hun-
gered go.
Madness shall be on the people, ghastly jealousies
arise;
Brother's blood shall cry on brother up the dead
and empty skies.

"I will burn and dig and hack
Till the heavens suffer lack;
God shall feel a pleasure fail him, crying to his
cherubim,
'Who hath flung yon mud-ball there
Where my world went green and fair?'
I shall laugh and hug me, hearing how his senti-
nels declare,

"'T is the Brute they chained to labor! He has made the bright earth dim.
Store of wares and pelf a plenty, but they got no good of him.'"

So he plotted in his rage:
So he deals it, age by age.
But even as he roared his curse a still small Voice befell;
Lo, a still and pleasant voice bade them none the less rejoice,
For the Brute must bring the good time on; he has no other choice.
He may struggle, sweat, and yell, but he knows exceeding well
He must work them out salvation ere they send him back to hell.

All the desert that he made
He must treble bless with shade,
In primal wastes set precious seed of rapture and of pain;
All the strongholds that he built
For the powers of greed and guilt —
He must strew their bastions down the sea and choke their towers with silt;

He must make the temples clean for the gods to
come again,
And lift the lordly cities under skies without a
stain.

In a very cunning tether
He must lead the tyrant weather;
He must loose the curse of Adam from the worn
neck of the race;
He must cast out hate and fear,
Dry away each fruitless tear,
And make the fruitful tears to gush from the deep
heart and clear.
He must give each man his portion, each his
pride and worthy place;
He must batter down the arrogant and lift the
weary face,
On each vile mouth set purity, on each low fore-
head grace.

Then, perhaps, at the last day,
They will whistle him away,
Lay a hand upon his muzzle in the face of God,
and say,
"Honor, Lord, the Thing we tamed!
Let him not be scourged or blamed.

Even through his wrath and fierceness was thy
fierce wroth world reclaimed!
Honor Thou thy servants' servant; let thy justice now be shown."
Then the Lord will heed their saying, and the
Brute come to his own,
'Twixt the Lion and the Eagle, by the armpost
of the Throne.

THE MENAGERIE

THANK God my brain is not inclined to cut
Such capers every day! I 'm just about
Mellow, but then — There goes the tent-flap shut.
Rain 's in the wind. I thought so: every snout
Was twitching when the keeper turned me out.

That screaming parrot makes my blood run cold.
Gabriel's trump! the big bull elephant
Squeals "Rain!" to the parched herd. The monkeys scold,
And jabber that it 's rain water they want.
(It makes me sick to see a monkey pant.)

I 'll foot it home, to try and make believe
I 'm sober. After this I stick to beer,
And drop the circus when the sane folks leave.
A man 's a fool to look at things too near:
They look back, and begin to cut up queer.

Beasts do, at any rate; especially
Wild devils caged. They have the coolest way

Of being something else than what you see:
You pass a sleek young zebra nosing hay,
A nylghau looking bored and distingué, —

And think you 've seen a donkey and a bird.
Not on your life! Just glance back, if you
dare.
The zebra chews, the nylghau has n't stirred;
But something 's happened, Heaven knows what
or where,
To freeze your scalp and pompadour your hair.

I 'm not precisely an æolian lute
Hung in the wandering winds of sentiment,
But drown me if the ugliest, meanest brute
Grunting and fretting in that sultry tent
Did n't just floor me with embarrassment!

'T was like a thunder-clap from out the clear, —
One minute they were circus beasts, some grand,
Some ugly, some amusing, and some queer:
Rival attractions to the hobo band,
The flying jenny, and the peanut stand.

Next minute they were old hearth-mates of mine!
Lost people, eyeing me with such a stare!
Patient, satiric, devilish, divine;

A gaze of hopeless envy, squalid care,
Hatred, and thwarted love, and dim despair.

Within my blood my ancient kindred spoke,—
Grotesque and monstrous voices, heard afar
Down ocean caves when behemoth awoke,
Or through fern forests roared the plesiosaur
Locked with the giant-bat in ghastly war.

And suddenly, as in a flash of light,
I saw great Nature working out her plan;
Through all her shapes from mastodon to mite
Forever groping, testing, passing on
To find at last the shape and soul of Man.

Till in the fullness of accomplished time,
Comes brother Forepaugh, upon business bent,
Tracks her through frozen and through torrid clime,
And shows us, neatly labeled in a tent,
The stages of her huge experiment;

Blabbing aloud her shy and reticent hours;
Dragging to light her blinking, slothful moods;
Publishing fretful seasons when her powers
Worked wild and sullen in her solitudes,
Or when her mordant laughter shook the woods.

Here, round about me, were her vagrant births;
Sick dreams she had, fierce projects she essayed;
Her qualms, her fiery prides, her crazy mirths;
The troublings of her spirit as she strayed,
Cringed, gloated, mocked, was lordly, was afraid,

On that long road she went to seek mankind;
Here were the darkling coverts that she beat
To find the Hider she was sent to find;
Here the distracted footprints of her feet
Whereby her soul's Desire she came to greet.

But why should they, her botch-work, turn about
And stare disdain at me, her finished job?
Why was the place one vast suspended shout
Of laughter? Why did all the daylight throb
With soundless guffaw and dumb-stricken sob?

Helpless I stood among those awful cages;
The beasts were walking loose, and I was bagged!
I, I, last product of the toiling ages,
Goal of heroic feet that never lagged,—
A little man in trousers, slightly jagged.

Deliver me from such another jury!
The Judgment-day will be a picnic to 't.
Their satire was more dreadful than their fury,

And worst of all was just a kind of brute
Disgust, and giving up, and sinking mute.

Survival of the fittest, adaptation,
And all their other evolution terms,
Seem to omit one small consideration,
To wit, that tumblebugs and angleworms
Have souls: there 's soul in everything that squirms.

And souls are restless, plagued, impatient things,
All dream and unaccountable desire;
Crawling, but pestered with the thought of wings;
Spreading through every inch of earth's old mire
Mystical hanker after something higher.

Wishes *are* horses, as I understand.
I guess a wistful polyp that has strokes
Of feeling faint to gallivant on land
Will come to be a scandal to his folks;
Legs he will sprout, in spite of threats and jokes.

And at the core of every life that crawls
Or runs or flies or swims or vegetates —
Churning the mammoth's heart-blood, in the galls
Of shark and tiger planting gorgeous hates,
Lighting the love of eagles for their mates;

Yes, in the dim brain of the jellied fish
That is and is not living — moved and stirred
From the beginning a mysterious wish,
A vision, a command, a fatal Word:
The name of Man was uttered, and they heard.

Upward along the æons of old war
They sought him: wing and shank-bone, claw
and bill
Were fashioned and rejected; wide and far
They roamed the twilight jungles of their will;
But still they sought him, and desired him still.

Man they desired, but mind you, Perfect Man,
The radiant and the loving, yet to be!
I hardly wonder, when they came to scan
The upshot of their strenuosity,
They gazed with mixed emotions upon *me*.

Well, my advice to you is, Face the creatures,
Or spot them sideways with your weather eye,
Just to keep tab on their expansive features;
It is n't pleasant when you 're stepping high
To catch a giraffe smiling on the sly.

If nature made you graceful, don't get gay
Back-to before the hippopotamus;

If meek and godly, find some place to play
Besides right where three mad hyenas fuss:
You may hear language that we won't discuss.

If you 're a sweet thing in a flower-bed hat,
Or her best fellow with your tie tucked in,
Don't squander love's bright springtime girding at
An old chimpanzee with an Irish chin:
There may be hidden meaning in his grin.

THE GOLDEN JOURNEY

All day he drowses by the sail
With dreams of her, and all night long
The broken waters are at song
Of how she lingers, wild and pale,
When all the temple lights are dumb,
And weaves her spells to make him come.

The wide sea traversed, he will stand
With straining eyes, until the shoal
Green water from the prow shall roll
Upon the yellow strip of sand —
Searching some fern-hid tangled way
Into the forest old and grey.

Then he will leap upon the shore,
And cast one look up at the sun,
Over his loosened locks will run
The dawn breeze, and a bird will pour
Its rapture out to make life seem
Too sweet to leave for such a dream.

But all the swifter will he go
Through the pale, scattered asphodels,
Down mote-hung dusk of olive dells,
To where the ancient basins throw
Fleet threads of blue and trembling zones
Of gold upon the temple stones.

There noon keeps just a twilight trace;
Twixt love and hate, and death and birth,
No man may choose; nor sobs nor mirth
May enter in that haunted place.
All day the fountain sphynx lets drip
Slow drops of silence from her lip.

To hold the porch-roof slender girls
Of milk-white marble stand arow;
Doubt never blurs a single brow,
And never the noon's faintness curls
From their expectant hush of pride
The lips the god has glorified.

But these things he will barely view,
Or if he stay to heed them, still
But as the lark the lights that spill
From out the sun it soars unto,
Where, past the splendors and the heats,
The sun's heart's self forever beats.

For wide the brazen doors will swing
Soon as his sandals touch the pave;
The anxious light inside will wave
And tremble to a lunar ring
About the form that lieth prone
Before the dreadful altar-stone.

She will not look or speak or stir,
But with drowned lips and cheeks death-white
Will lie amid the pool of light,
Until, grown faint with thirst of her,
He shall bow down his face and sink
Breathless beneath the eddying brink.

Then a swift music will begin,
And as the brazen doors shut slow,
There will be hurrying to and fro,
And lights and calls and silver din,
While through the star-freaked swirl of air
The god's sweet cruel eyes will stare.

HEART'S WILD-FLOWER

TO-NIGHT her lids shall lift again, slow, soft, with
vague desire,
And lay about my breast and brain their hush of
spirit fire,
And I shall take the sweet of pain as the laborer
his hire.

And though no word shall e'er be said to ease the
ghostly sting,
And though our hearts, unhoused, unfed, must
still go wandering,
My sign is set upon her head while stars do meet
and sing.

Not such a sign as women wear who make their
foreheads tame
With life's long tolerance, and bear love's sweet-
est, humblest name,
Nor such as passion eateth bare with its crown
of tears and flame.

Nor such a sign as happy friend sets on his
friend's dear brow

When meadow-pipings break and blend to a key
of autumn woe,
And the woodland says playtime 's at end, best
unclasp hands and go.

But where she strays, through blight or blooth,
one fadeless flower she wears,
A little gift God gave my youth, — whose petals
dim were fears,
Awes, adorations, songs of ruth, hesitancies, and
tears.

O heart of mine, with all thy powers of white
beatitude,
What are the dearest of God's dowers to the
children of his blood?
How blow the shy, shy wilding flowers in the
hollows of his wood?

HARMONICS

This string upon my harp was best beloved:
I thought I knew its secrets through and through;
Till an old man, whose young eyes lightened blue
'Neath his white hair, bent over me and moved
His fingers up and down, and broke the wire
To such a laddered music, rung on rung,
As from the patriarch's pillow skyward sprung
Crowded with wide-flung wings and feet of fire.

O vibrant heart! so metely tuned and strung
That any untaught hand can draw from thee
One clear gold note that makes the tired years
    young—
What of the time when Love had whispered me
Where slept thy nodes, and my hand pausefully
Gave to the dim harmonics voice and tongue?

ON THE RIVER

THE faint stars wake and wonder,
Fade and find heart anew;
Above us and far under
Sphereth the watchful blue.

Silent she sits, outbending,
A wild pathetic grace,
A beauty strange, heart-rending,
Upon her hair and face.

O spirit cries that sever
The cricket's level drone!
O to give o'er endeavor
And let love have its own!

Within the mirrored bushes
There wakes a little stir;
The white-throat moves, and hushes
Her nestlings under her.

Beneath, the lustrous river,
The watchful sky o'erhead.
God, God, that Thou should'st ever
Poison thy children's bread!

THE BRACELET OF GRASS

The opal heart of afternoon
Was clouding on to throbs of storm,
Ashen within the ardent west
The lips of thunder muttered harm,
And as a bubble like to break
Hung heaven's trembling amethyst,
When with the sedge-grass by the lake
I braceleted her wrist.

And when the ribbon grass was tied,
Sad with the happiness we planned,
Palm linked in palm we stood awhile
And watched the raindrops dot the sand;
Until the anger of the breeze
Chid all the lake's bright breathing down,
And ravished all the radiancies
From her deep eyes of brown.

We gazed from shelter on the storm,
And through our hearts swept ghostly pain
To see the shards of day sweep past,
Broken, and none might mend again.

Broken, that none shall ever mend;
Loosened, that none shall ever tie.
O the wind and the wind, will it never end?
O the sweeping past of the ruined sky!

THE DEPARTURE

I

I SAT beside the glassy evening sea,
One foot upon the thin horn of my lyre,
And all its strings of laughter and desire
Crushed in the rank wet grasses heedlessly;
Nor did my dull eyes care to question how
The boat close by had spread its saffron sails,
Nor what might mean the coffers and the bales,
And streaks of new wine on the gilded prow.
Neither was wonder in me when I saw
Fair women step therein, though they were fair
Even to adoration and to awe,
And in the gracious fillets of their hair
Were blossoms from a garden I had known,
Sweet mornings ere the apple buds were blown.

II

One gazed steadfast into the dying west
With lips apart to greet the evening star;
And one with eyes that caught the strife and jar
Of the sea's heart, followed the sunward breast

Of a lone gull; from a slow harp one drew
Blind music like a laugh or like a wail;
And in the uncertain shadow of the sail
One wove a crown of berries and of yew.
Yet even as I said with dull desire,
"All these were mine, and one was mine indeed,"
The smoky music burst into a fire,
And I was left alone in my great need,
One foot upon the thin horn of my lyre
And all its strings crushed in the dripping weed.

FADED PICTURES

Only two patient eyes to stare
Out of the canvas. All the rest —
The warm green gown, the small hands pressed
Light in the lap, the braided hair

That must have made the sweet low brow
So earnest, centuries ago,
When some one saw it change and glow —
All faded! Just the eyes burn now.

I dare say people pass and pass
Before the blistered little frame,
And dingy work without a name
Stuck in behind its square of glass.

But I, well, I left Raphael
Just to come drink these eyes of hers,
To think away the stains and blurs
And make all new again and well.

Only, for tears my head will bow,
Because there on my heart's last wall,
Scarce one tint left to tell it all,
A picture keeps its eyes, somehow.

A GREY DAY

Grey drizzling mists the moorlands drape,
Rain whitens the dead sea,
From headland dim to sullen cape
Grey sails creep wearily.
I know not how that merchantman
Has found the heart; but 't is her plan
Seaward her endless course to shape.

Unreal as insects that appall
A drunkard's peevish brain,
O'er the grey deep the dories crawl,
Four-legged, with rowers twain:
Midgets and minims of the earth,
Across old ocean's vasty girth
Toiling — heroic, comical!

I wonder how that merchant's crew
Have ever found the will!
I wonder what the fishers do
To keep them toiling still!
I wonder how the heart of man
Has patience to live out its span,
Or wait until its dreams come true.

THE RIDE BACK

Before the coming of the dark, he dreamed
An old-world faded story: of a knight,
Much like in need to him, who was no knight!
And of a road, much like the road his soul
Groped over, desperate to meet Her soul.
Beside the bed Death waited. And he dreamed.

His limbs were heavy from the fight,
His mail was dark with dust and blood;
On his good horse they bound him tight,
And on his breast they bound the rood
To help him in the ride that night.

When he crashed through the wood's wet rim,
About the dabbled reeds a breeze
Went moaning broken words and dim;
The haggard shapes of twilight trees
Caught with their scrawny hands at him.

Between the doubtful aisles of day
Strange folk and lamentable stood

To maze and beckon him astray,
But through the grey wrath of the wood
He held right on his bitter way.

When he came where the trees were thin,
The moon sat waiting there to see;
On her worn palm she laid her chin,
And laughed awhile in sober glee
To think how strong this knight had been.

When he rode past the pallid lake,
The withered yellow stems of flags
Stood breast-high for his horse to break;
Lewd as the palsied lips of hags
The petals in the moon did shake.

When he came by the mountain wall,
The snow upon the heights looked down
And said, "The sight is pitiful.
The nostrils of his steed are brown
With frozen blood; and he will fall."

The iron passes of the hills
With question were importunate;
And, but the sharp-tongued icy rills
Had grown for once compassionate,
The spiteful shades had had their wills.

Just when the ache in breast and brain
And the frost smiting at his face
Had sealed his spirit up with pain,
He came out in a better place,
And morning lay across the plain.

He saw the wet snails crawl and cling
On fern-stalks where the rime had run,
The careless birds went wing and wing,
And in the low smile of the sun
Life seemed almost a pleasant thing.

Right on the panting charger swung
Through the bright depths of quiet grass;
The knight's lips moved as if they sung,
And through the peace there came to pass
The flattery of lute and tongue.

From the mid-flowering of the mead
There swelled a sob of minstrelsy,
Faint sackbuts and the dreamy reed,
And plaintive lips of maids thereby,
And songs blown out like thistle seed.

Forth from her maidens came the bride,
And as his loosened rein fell slack

He muttered, "In their throats they lied
Who said that I should ne'er win back
To kiss her lips before I died!"

SONG–FLOWER AND POPPY

I

IN NEW YORK

HE plays the deuce with my writing time,
For the penny my sixth-floor neighbor throws;
He finds me proud of my pondered rhyme,
And he leaves me — well, God knows
It takes the shine from a tunester's line
When a little mate of the deathless Nine
Pipes up under your nose!

For listen, there is his voice again,
Wistful and clear and piercing sweet.
Where did the boy find such a strain
To make a dead heart beat?
And how in the name of care can he bear
To jet such a fountain into the air
In this gray gulch of a street?

Tuscan slopes or the Piedmontese?
Umbria under the Apennine?

South, where the terraced lemon-trees
Round rich Sorrento shine?
Venice moon on the smooth lagoon? —
Where have I heard that aching tune,
That boyish throat divine?

Beyond my roofs and chimney pots
A rag of sunset crumbles gray;
Below, fierce radiance hangs in clots
O'er the streams that never stay.
Shrill and high, newsboys cry
The worst of the city's infamy
For one more sordid day.

But my desire has taken sail
For lands beyond, soft-horizoned:
Down languorous leagues I hold the trail,
From Marmalada, steeply throned
Above high pastures washed with light,
Where dolomite by dolomite
Looms sheer and spectral-coned,

To purple vineyards looking south
On reaches of the still Tyrrhene;
Virgilian headlands, and the mouth
Of Tiber, where that ship put in
To take the dead men home to God,

Whereof Casella told the mode
To the great Florentine.

Up stairways blue with flowering weed
I climb to hill-hung Bergamo;
All day I watch the thunder breed
Golden above the springs of Po,
Till the voice makes sure its wavering lure,
And by Assisi's portals pure
I stand, with heart bent low.

O hear, how it blooms in the blear dayfall,
That flower of passionate wistful song!
How it blows like a rose by the iron wall
Of the city loud and strong.
How it cries "Nay, nay" to the worldling's way,
To the heart's clear dream how it whispers, "Yea;
Time comes, though the time is long."

Beyond my roofs and chimney piles
Sunset crumbles, ragged, dire;
The roaring street is hung for miles
With fierce electric fire.
Shrill and high, newsboys cry
The gross of the planet's destiny
Through one more sullen gyre.

Stolidly the town flings down
Its lust by day for its nightly lust;
Who does his given stint, 't is known,
Shall have his mug and crust.—
Too base of mood, too harsh of blood,
Too stout to seize the grosser good,
Too hungry after dust!

O hark! how it blooms in the falling dark,
That flower of mystical yearning song:
Sad as a hermit thrush, as a lark
Uplifted, glad, and strong.
Heart, we have chosen the better part!
Save sacred love and sacred art
Nothing is good for long.

II

AT ASSISI

Before St. Francis' burg I wait,
Frozen in spirit, faint with dread;
His presence stands within the gate,
Mild splendor rings his head.
Gently he seems to welcome me:
Knows he not I am quick, and he
Is dead, and priest of the dead?

I turn away from the gray church pile;
I dare not enter, thus undone:
Here in the roadside grass awhile
I will lie and watch for the sun.
Too purged of earth's good glee and strife,
Too drained of the honied lusts of life,
Was the peace these old saints won!

And lo! how the laughing earth says no
To the fear that mastered me;
To the blood that aches and clamors so
How it whispers "Verily."

Here by my side, marvelous-dyed,
Bold stray-away from the courts of pride,
A poppy-bell flaunts free.

St. Francis sleeps upon his hill,
And a poppy flower laughs down his creed;
Triumphant light her petals spill,
His shrines are dim indeed.
Men build and plan, but the soul of man,
Coming with haughty eyes to scan,
Feels richer, wilder need.

How long, old builder Time, wilt bide
Till at thy thrilling word
Life's crimson pride shall have to bride
The spirit's white accord,
Within that gate of good estate
Which thou must build us soon or late,
Hoar workman of the Lord?

HOW THE MEAD-SLAVE WAS SET FREE

Nay, move not! Sit just as you are,
Under the carved wings of the chair.
The hearth-glow sifting through your hair
Turns every dim pearl to a star
Dawn-drowned in floods of brightening air.

I have been thinking of that night
When all the wide hall burst to blaze
With spears caught up, thrust fifty ways
To find my throat, while I lay white
And sick with joy, to think the days

I dragged out in your hateful North —
A slave, constrained at banquet's need
To fill the black bull's horns with mead
For drunken sea-thieves — were henceforth
Cast from me as a poison weed,

While Death thrust roses in my hands!
But you, who knew the flowers he had
Were no such roses ripe and glad

As nod in my far southern lands,
But pallid things to make men sad,

Put back the spears with one calm hand,
Raised on your knee my wondering head,
Wiped off the trickling drops of red
From my torn forehead with a strand
Of your bright loosened hair, and said:

"Sea-rovers! would you kill a skald?
This boy has hearkened Odin sing
Unto the clang and winnowing
Of raven's wings. His heart is thralled
To music, as to some strong king;

"And this great thraldom works disdain
Of lesser serving. Once release
These bonds he bears, and he may please
To give you guerdon sweet as rain
To sailors calmed in thirsty seas."

Then, having soothed their rage to rest,
You led me to old Skagi's throne,
Where yellow gold rims in the stone;
And in my arms, against my breast,
Thrust his great harp of walrus bone.

How they came crowding, tunes on tunes!
How good it was to touch the strings
And feel them thrill like happy things
That flutter from the gray cocoons
On hedge rows, in your gradual springs!

All grew a blur before my sight,
As when the stealthy white fog slips
At noonday on the staggering ships;
I saw one single spot of light,
Your white face, with its eager lips —

And so I sang to that. O thou
Who liftedst me from out my shame!
Wert thou content when Skagi came,
Put his own chaplet on my brow,
And bent and kissed his own harp-frame?

A DIALOGUE IN PURGATORY

Poi disse un altro . . . . " Io son Buonconte :
Giovanna o altri non ha di me cura ;
Per ch' io vo tra costor con bassa fronte."

Seguito il terzo spirito al secondo,
" Ricorditi di me, che son la Pia ;
Siena mi fe, disfecemi Maremma.
Salsi colui che inannellata pria
Disposata m' avea colla sua gemma."

PURGATORIO, CANTO V.

I

BUONCONTE

SISTER, the sun has ceased to shine ;
By companies of twain and trine
Stars gather ; from the sea
The moon comes momently.

On all the roads that ring our hill
The sighing and the hymns are still :
It is our time to gain
Strength for to-morrow's pain.

Yet still your eyes are wholly bent
Upon the way that Virgil went,
Following Sordello's sign,
With the dark Florentine.

Night now has barred their upward track :
There where the mountain-side folds back
And in the Vale of Flowers
The Princes count their hours

Those three friends sit in the clear starlight
With the green-clad angels left and right, —
Soul made by wakeful soul
More earnest for the goal.

So let us, sister, though our place
Is barren of that Valley's grace,
Sit hand in hand, till we
Seem rich as those friends be.

II

LA PIA

Brother, 't were sweet your hand to feel
In mine; it would a little heal
The shame that makes me poor,
And dumb at the heart's core.

But where our spirits felt Love's dearth,
Down on the green and pleasant earth,
Remains the fleshly shell,
Love's garment tangible.

So now our hands have naught to say:
Heart unto heart some other way
Must utter forth its pain,
Must glee or comfort gain.

Ah, no! For souls like you and me
Some comfort waits, but never glee:
Not yours the young men's singing
In Heaven, at the bride-bringing;

Not mine, beside God's living waters,
Dance of the marriageable daughters,
The laughter and the ease
Beneath His summer trees.

III

BUONCONTE

In fair Arezzo's halls and bowers
My Giovanna speeds her hours
Delicately, nor cares
To shorten by her prayers

My days upon this mount of ruth:
If those who come from earth speak sooth,
Though still I call and call,
She does not heed at all.

And if aright your words I read
At Dante's passing, he you wed
Dipped from the drains of Hell
The marriage hydromel.

O therefore, while the moon intense
Holds yonder dreaming sea suspense,
And round the shadowy coasts
Gather the wistful ghosts,

Let us sit quiet all the night,
And wonder, wonder on the light
Worn by those spirits fair
Whom Love has not left bare.

IV

LA PIA

Even as theirs, the chance was mine
To meet and mate beneath Love's sign,
To feel in soul and sense
The solemn influence

Which, breathed upon a man or maid,
Maketh forever unafraid,
Though life with death unite
That spirit to affright, —

Which lifts the changèd heart high up,
As the priest lifts the changèd cup,
Boldens the feet to pace
Before God's proving face.

O just a thought beyond the blue
The wings of the dove yearned down and through!
Even now I hear and hear
How near they were, how near!

I murmur not. Rightly disgraced,
The weak hand stretched abroad in haste
For gifts barely allowed
The tacit, strong, and proud.

But therefore was I so intent
To watch where Dante onward went
With the Roman spirit pure
And the grave troubadour,

Because my mind was busy then
With the loves that wait those gentle men:

Cunizza one; and one
Bice, above the sun;

And for the other, more and less
Than woman's near-felt tenderness,
A million voices dim
Praising him, praising him.

V

BUONCONTE

The waves that wash this mountain's base
Were crimson in the sun's low rays,
When, singing high and fast,
An angel downward passed,

To bid some patient soul arise
And make it fair for Paradise;
And upward, so attended,
That soul its journey wended;

Yet you, who in these lower rings
Wait for the coming of such wings,
Turned not your eyes to view
Whether they came for you,

But watched, but watched great Virgil stayed
Greeting Sordello's couchant shade,

Which to salute him rose
Like lion from its pose;

While humbly by those lords of song
Stood he whose living limbs are strong
To mount where Mary's bliss
Is shed on Beatrice.

On him your gaze was fastened, more
Than on those great names Mantua bore;
Your eyes hold the distress
Still, of that wistfulness.

Yea, fit he seemed much love to rouse!
His pilgrim lips and iron brows
Grew like a woman's, dim,
While you held speech with him;

And troubled came his mortal breath
The while I told him of my death;
His looks were changed and wan
When Virgil led him on.

VI

LA PIA

E'er since Casella came this morn,
Newly o'er yonder ocean borne,

Bound upward for the choir
Who purge themselves in fire,

And from that meinie he was of
Stayed backward at my cry of love,
To speak awhile with me
Of life and Tuscany,

And, parting, told us how e'er day
Was done, Dante would come this way,
With mortal feet, to find
His sweetheart, sky-enshrined,—

E'er since Casella spoke such news
My heart has lain in a golden muse,
Picturing him and her,
What starry ones they were.

And now the moon sheds its compassion
O'er the hushed mount, I try to fashion
The manner of their meeting,
Their few first words of greeting.

O well for them, with claspèd hands,
Unshamed amid the heavenly bands!
They hear no pitying pair
Of old-time lovers there

Look down and say in an undertone,
" This latest-come, who comes alone,
Was still alone on earth,
And lonely from his birth."

Nor feel a sudden whisper mar
God's weather, " Dost thou see the scar
That spirit hideth so ?
Who dealt her such a blow

" That God can hardly wipe it out ? "
And answer, " She gave love, no doubt,
To one who saw not fit
To set much store by it."

THE DAGUERREOTYPE

This, then, is she,
My mother as she looked at seventeen,
When she first met my father. Young incredibly,
Younger than spring, without the faintest trace
Of disappointment, weariness, or tean
Upon the childlike earnestness and grace
Of the waiting face.
These close-wound ropes of pearl
(Or common beads made precious by their use)
Seem heavy for so slight a throat to wear;
But the low bodice leaves the shoulders bare
And half the glad swell of the breast, for news
That now the woman stirs within the girl.
And yet,
Even so, the loops and globes
Of beaten gold
And jet
Hung, in the stately way of old,
From the ears' drooping lobes
On festivals and Lord's-day of the week,
Show all too matron-sober for the cheek,—

Which, now I look again, is perfect child,
Or no — or no — 't is girlhood's very self,
Moulded by some deep, mischief-ridden elf
So meek, so maiden mild,
But startling the close gazer with the sense
Of passions forest-shy and forest-wild,
And delicate delirious merriments.

As a moth beats sidewise
And up and over, and tries
To skirt the irresistible lure
Of the flame that has him sure,
My spirit, that is none too strong to-day,
Flutters and makes delay, —
Pausing to wonder on the perfect lips,
Lifting to muse upon the low-drawn hair
And each hid radiance there,
But powerless to stem the tide-race bright,
The vehement peace which drifts it toward the light
Where soon — ah, now, with cries
Of grief and giving-up unto its gain
It shrinks no longer nor denies,
But dips
Hurriedly home to the exquisite heart of pain, —
And all is well, for I have seen them plain,
The unforgettable, the unforgotten eyes!

Across the blinding gush of these good tears
They shine as in the sweet and heavy years
When by her bed and chair
We children gathered jealously to share
The sunlit aura breathing myrrh and thyme,
Where the sore-stricken body made a clime
Gentler than May and pleasanter than rhyme,
Holier and more mystical than prayer.

God, how thy ways are strange!
That this should be, even this,
The patient head
Which suffered years ago the dreary change!
That these so dewy lips should be the same
As those I stooped to kiss
And heard my harrowing half-spoken name,
A little ere the one who bowed above her,
Our father and her very constant lover,
Rose stoical, and we knew that she was dead.
Then I, who could not understand or share
His antique nobleness,
Being unapt to bear
The insults which time flings us for our proof,
Fled from the horrible roof
Into the alien sunshine merciless,
The shrill satiric fields ghastly with day,
Raging to front God in his pride of sway

And hurl across the lifted swords of fate
That ringed Him where He sat
My puny gage of scorn and desolate hate
Which somehow should undo Him, after all!
That this girl face, expectant, virginal,
Which gazes out at me
Boon as a sweetheart, as if nothing loth
(Save for the eyes, with other presage stored)
To pledge me troth,
And in the kingdom where the heart is lord
Take sail on the terrible gladness of the deep
Whose winds the gray Norns keep, —
That this should be indeed
The flesh which caught my soul, a flying seed,
Out of the to and fro
Of scattering hands where the seedsman Mage,
Stooping from star to star and age to age
Sings as he sows!
That underneath this breast
Nine moons I fed
Deep of divine unrest,
While over and over in the dark she said,
"Blessèd! but not as happier children blessed"—
That this should be
Even she. . . .
God, how with time and change
Thou makest thy footsteps strange!

Ah, now I know
They play upon me, and it is not so.
Why, 't is a girl I never saw before,
A little thing to flatter and make weep,
To tease until her heart is sore,
Then kiss and clear the score;
A gypsy run-the-fields,
A little liberal daughter of the earth,
Good for what hour of truancy and mirth
The careless season yields
Hither-side the flood o' the year and yonder of the neap;
Then thank you, thanks again, and twenty light good-byes. —
O shrined above the skies,
Frown not, clear brow,
Darken not, holy eyes!
Thou knowest well I know that it is thou!
Only to save me from such memories
As would unman me quite,
Here in this web of strangeness caught
And prey to troubled thought
Do I devise
These foolish shifts and slight;
Only to shield me from the afflicting sense
Of some waste influence
Which from this morning face and lustrous hair
Breathes on me sudden ruin and despair.

In any other guise,
With any but this girlish depth of gaze,
Your coming had not so unsealed and poured
The dusty amphoras where I had stored
The drippings of the winepress of my days.
I think these eyes foresee,
Now in their unawakened virgin time,
Their mother's pride in me,
And dream even now, unconsciously,
Upon each soaring peak and sky-hung lea
You pictured I should climb.
Broken premonitions come,
Shapes, gestures visionary,
Not as once to maiden Mary
The manifest angel with fresh lilies came
Intelligibly calling her by name;
But vanishingly, dumb,
Thwarted and bright and wild,
As heralding a sin-defiled,
Earth-encumbered, blood-begotten, passionate man-child,
Who yet should be a trump of mighty call
Blown in the gates of evil kings
To make them fall;
Who yet should be a sword of flame before
The soul's inviolate door
To beat away the clang of hellish wings;

Who yet should be a lyre
Of high unquenchable desire
In the day of little things. —
Look, where the amphoras,
The yield of many days,
Trod by my hot soul from the pulp of self
And set upon the shelf
In sullen pride
The Vineyard-master's tasting to abide —
O mother mine!
Are these the bringings-in, the doings fine,
Of him you used to praise?
Emptied and overthrown
The jars lie strown.
These, for their flavor duly nursed,
Drip from the stopples vinegar accursed;
These, I thought honied to the very seal,
Dry, dry, — a little acid meal,
A pinch of mouldy dust,
Sole leavings of the amber-mantling must;
These, rude to look upon,
But flasking up the liquor dearest won,
Through sacred hours and hard,
With watching and with wrestlings and with grief,
Even of these, of these in chief,
The stale breath sickens, reeking from the shard.

Nothing is left. Ay, how much less than
naught!
What shall be said or thought
Of the slack hours and waste imaginings,
The cynic rending of the wings,
Known to that froward, that unreckoning heart
Whereof this brewage was the precious part,
Treasured and set away with furtive boast?
O dear and cruel ghost,
Be merciful, be just!
See, I was yours and I am in the dust.
Then look not so, as if all things were well!
Take your eyes from me, leave me to my shame,
Or else, if gaze they must,
Steel them with judgment, darken them with
blame;
But by the ways of light ineffable
You bade me go and I have faltered from,
By the low waters moaning out of hell
Whereto my feet have come,
Lay not on me these intolerable
Looks of rejoicing love, of pride, of happy trust!

Nothing dismayed?
By all I say and all I hint not made
Afraid?
O then, stay by me! Let
These eyes afflict me, cleanse me, keep me yet.

Brave eyes and true!
See how the shriveled heart, that long has lain
Dead to delight and pain,
Stirs, and begins again
To utter pleasant life, as if it knew
The wintry days were through;
As if in its awakening boughs it heard
The quick, sweet-spoken bird.
Strong eyes and brave,
Inexorable to save!

www.ingramcontent.com/pod-product-compliance
Lightning Source LLC
LaVergne TN
LVHW021427110826
845150LV00007B/2122

* 9 7 8 1 4 2 5 5 0 7 5 4 1 *